DIVINE DELIVERANCE
Henry Leon McNeil
Royalty Kingdom Publishing

Published by Royalty Kingdom Publishing

To request permission, contact the publisher at
info@royaltykingdompublishing.com
ISBN: 979-8-9876106-1-9
LCCN: 9798987610619

DIVINE DELIVERANCE: A BOOK OF MIRACLES

Table of Contents

INTRODUCTION

As I contemplated writing about the various miracles that have taken place in my life, I had to first realize that when God saves you from destruction, be it physical, psychological, or spiritual. His salvation has a basic and specific purpose. The basic purpose of any miracle happening in your life is that God will be glorified. This premise is found throughout scripture.

We know from scripture that we are to tell of our deliverance.

Psalms 119:46: "I will speak of thy testimonies also before kings, and will not be ashamed. "

The scripture also reminds us that affliction is a necessary and uncomfortable thing.

Psalms 119:71: "It is good for me that I have been afflicted; that I might learn thy statutes."

Even though we find affliction painful, it is nevertheless one of God's ways of getting our attention. The same is true for those traumatic and sometimes very painful incidents that occur in our lives. Such events and happenings will cause you to go down on bended knees and call on God in a manner like you have never experienced before. Our painful experiences tend to drive us to our knees, or they will cause us to pray and ask God for help, no matter what position we might be physically in, as seen in the first miracle I discussed in this book.

Henry Leon McNeil

To further explain what David must have been talking about with the comment on affliction, you can see that in such a state, you have more time to read the word of God. And as such, you get to spend quality time touching God and learning his statutes. We know that when you read scripture, you are touching God because the bible tells us so.

John 1:1 (KJV) 1, In the beginning, was the Word, and the Word was God, and the Word was with God.

Consequently, when we study the Bible, we study our Lord and Savior, Jesus Christ. Remember that what satan meant for your harm will often be turned into a blessing by God. Only God is in complete control of the world. Satan is not a creator; instead, he was created by God. And as such, God will allow him to cause great trials and tests that ultimately show the power of God when we, through faith in God the Father, Son, and the Holy Ghost, are delivered from Satan's fiery darts.

Just remember, our trials, tests, and tribulations are never out of God's rescue reach. We must understand that our lives are not our own. We were created by the great "I Am" to work in God's vineyard. In essence, we need to adhere to God's purpose for us and not yield to our fleshly feelings.

I'm writing about three different and distinct deliveries or divine rescues that our God and Savior,

Jesus Christ, worked on my behalf individually. These events helped shape the landscape of the faith and trust I am now endowed with. The following is a summary of how God moved me to use the skill set He had planted deep into the crevices of my heart to achieve the unique God-inspired victories for each series of challenges identified in this book.

#1 FROM DOMESTIC ENTANGLEMENT

This particular incident in 1965 lasted less than three hours. Yet, it was one of the most dangerous 3 hours our young lives had ever experienced. In this very short time, my brother Sol and my two first cousins learned several valuable lessons, some of which we should have known already:

- Drinking to excess will usually cause the drinker to lose self-control, which can lead to a tragedy.
- No matter where you are, God is always present and can deliver you out of harm's way, even when you can't see how you will survive.
- God hears your prayer even when you are in an ungodly place.
- God will honor your vows even in those places.

Remember: you should never make vows with God and not keep them.

Deuteronomy 23:21 (KJV): When thou shalt vow a vow unto the Lord thy God, thou shalt not slack to pay it: for the Lord thy God will surely require it of thee; and it would be sin in thee.

When reading the details, you will see that God protected us in the midst of our unrighteous situation. All of our Christian parents were living at that time, and I believe that the hand of God protected us because of the prayers of our righteous parents.

James 5:16 (KJV). The effectual fervent prayer of a

Henry Leon McNeil

righteous man availeth much.

I have no doubt that St. John Baptist in Camden, Alabama, and our parents were praying for us, and these prayers caused God to deliver us from the clutches of wicked and vile recently released prisoners. The Lord will answer prayer.

#2 DIVINE DELIVERANCE IN VIETNAM

In 1970, my stay in Vietnam was precisely one year long. However, during that year, I experienced a multitude of difficulties, some of which were, in a word, insurmountable for me to pull through without the divine help of God. Getting out of Vietnam alive was something that I simply couldn't accomplish on my own. Several factors/situations caused my rescue;

- The timing had to be perfect. We know that no man's timing is perfect because perfect timing requires detailed knowledge of future events and all associated ramifications. No human has or ever will have such capabilities. God is the only one who can undertake and carry out such timing, especially during wartime situations.
- Knowing when and how to react to critical discourse. This is commonly known as "thinking perfectly on the fly."
- When reading the account of this deliverance, you will find that my simple mind discarded the

"Angelic" suggestion made by the payroll clerk to seek the safe job away from fighting fields and trade my fighting gun in for a powerful pencil in the NCO Club system. But when the clerk from the desk came outside of the office building to ask why I didn't want to simply approach the person in charge about pursuing a safe job I was well qualified for, I can honestly say that God caused me to pursue the best reaction to this critical discourse.

- Exercising faith and acquiring academic knowledge caused God's hand to move on the situation.

When I was questioned and quizzed by the NCO club officers and staff, God was in the mix and caused me to answer every question correctly. Nevertheless, these men were still not satisfied, even though I had satisfied all the academic and other necessary qualifications. It was very obvious to me, and I think it was known to the post commander, that they and the Major in charge of the Post Club system wanted to replace the outgoing accountant with a person of the same race. However, as God had set it up, there wasn't time to look for another replacement, and my unit was going deeper into the war field the next day. Consequently, at this point, they were forced

to accept me because of how God had set the whole matter up. God had created this entire situation in such a way that it had become too expensive for those who controlled the staffing to use the racist motif they had been searching for the last month, and the unit I was associated with was going to another country the next day. So, like it or not, they needed someone with my skill set, and that was that. LOOK AT GOD!

Getting re-assigned to a well-guarded command post protected by many gunships in the air and numerous Tanks and Armored Personnel carriers on the ground saved me from the death that my comrades went to the very same day I was transferred out of my Armored Cavalry Unit. I have no doubt that my home church in Camden, Alabama, and my parents were praying for me. The Lord will answer prayer.

Henry Leon McNeil

#3 DIVINE DELIVERANCE FROM STAGE 4 CANCER

There will be times when we wonder why we must go through particular situations at particular times. For example, when I was diagnosed with stage 4 colon cancer, I felt I was more obedient to God than I had ever been before. God called me into the preaching ministry years before I yielded to His calling. But in 1988, I responded to His call and started preaching the gospel of Jesus Christ. Going into the preaching ministry was no small matter for me. You see, I had observed the way my father had suffered at the hands of the various modern-day Pharisees situated in the New Testament church. Consequently, it was my opinion that I would never become a preacher of any kind, in any denomination, at any church or organization whatsoever, anywhere on earth. But I eventually discovered that such a decision didn't require my approval, even though it was my own body, used for the ministry.

1 Corinthians 6:19-20 (KJV) 19 Know ye not that your body is the temple of the Holy Ghost, which is in you, which ye have of God, and ye are not your own? 20 For ye are bought with a price: therefore, glorify God in your body, and in your spirit, which are God's.

And there you have it; God, in His infinite wisdom, determined I was to serve Him in the preaching ministry. And so, since I was now designated as one of God's representatives on the battlefield, I needed to make some changes. Trust me; there is a big difference between those trying to live a life dedicated

Henry Leon McNeil

to God's principles and concepts and those not operating in God's respective call on their life. When God calls us, he qualifies us for the battlefield we will face.

Romans 8:30 (KJV) 30 Moreover, whom he did predestinate, them he also called: and whom he called, them he also justified: and whom he justified, them he also glorified.

After the call, there are usually some lingering old habits and ways that we bring to our ministries that are not suited for the path God has destined for us. Consequently, we sometimes require mild or severe transformation to serve our present calling. Getting right to the point: In 1988, I answered the call to serve God in the ministry. In 1989, I joined the preaching cadre under Pastor W. C. Bunton's auspices and began learning the duties and ways of being a gospel minister for Jesus Christ. Then, in 1996, after serving eight years in the preaching ministry, I was called to God's pastoring ministry. However, there were many trials and rough spots in my life that needed smoothing out. After pastoring Mt. Olive Missionary Baptist Church in Dennison, Ohio, for two years, I was given a death sentence by my earthly doctor after he had examined me with various medical-type examinations, such as CAT scans, X-rays, and some tests I could not pronounce or spell.

Nevertheless, he and all his staff of medical experts were convinced beyond a shadow of a doubt that I had stage four colon cancer. Later, I'll go into the details of how I brought this issue to God in prayer. However, for this introductory part, I want you to

Henry Leon McNeil

know that even when we are obedient to God's Holy and righteous Word and His Holy and righteous will, for some of us, there is still a further cleansing step that God will order for your sainted path. There aren't many things in life that will solidify your relationship with God, like the pronouncement of an impending death sentence. This kind of fire causes us to look at our walk with God in a more serious and sober way.

This fire (stage 4 colon cancer) allowed me to reflect like the Hebrew boys. When King Nebuchadnezzar demanded they worship an idol god he had made or he would throw them into a fiery furnace, this was their response:

. Daniel 3:17-18 (KJV) "17 If it be so, our God whom we serve is able to deliver us from the burning fiery furnace, and he will deliver us out of thine hand, O king. 18 But if not, be it known unto thee, O king, that we will not serve thy gods, nor worship the golden image which thou hast set up.

Whenever Christians face insurmountable odds, we need to call on one who has never failed anyone. Now I knew, as did the Hebrew boys, that I might not physically survive the situation in my path, but I also knew, as did the Hebrew boys, that the God I served could deliver me if He so desired.

God healed me, and my surgeon acknowledged that, but for the supernatural powers of God, I couldn't have possibly been healed. To God be the glory!
God will sometimes allow his children to go through extreme adversity so that His glory might be manifested through you. Let me explain. In Paul's

second letter to the Corinthians, in 12:9, he records Jesus' answer to Paul's request for relief from a particular thorn in his side. Jesus answers: "My grace is sufficient for thee: for my strength is made perfect in weakness." Paraphrasing the passage, Jesus essentially says that your adversity opens up an opportunity for the world to witness My powers.

Moses was born in extreme adversity at a time when the pharaoh was trying to decrease the Jewish population. Consequently, he ordered the death of all Jewish male babies born. But God working through this adversity allowed Moses to escape and be adopted by the pharaoh's daughter. Ultimately, he led the Israelites out of Egyptian bondage and to the brink of the promised land of Canaan.

Gideon operated in extreme adversity, with 300 soldiers facing 135,000 Midianites. Oh, but God gave him the victory.

Elijah battled adversity when facing Ahab and his 400 false prophets on Mount Carmel. Oh, but God gave him the victory.

Finally, our Lord and Savior Jesus Christ was born in extreme adversity when King Herod had given orders that all Hebrew children two years old and younger in Bethlehem be killed. Through adversity, Jesus carried your sins and mine to the cross of Calvary. I am so glad that He came down through 42 generations so that I might have life and have it everlasting and more abundantly.

At the time of my impending death sentence from stage 4 colon cancer, my parents and most of the old Christian warriors of St. John in my hometown had already been "translated" to their heavenly mansion. However, my home church, Shiloh Baptist in Canton, Ohio, members from my former church, Shiloh Baptist in Pittsburgh, and many friends and kinfolks across the U.S.A. were all praying for my healing. When man has exhausted all efforts to bring about success, God is still in charge. He alone has the final say about everything, including your health and well-being. God healed me.

DIVINE DELIVERANCE FROM DOMESTIC ENTANGLEMENT IN 1965

Home Life and My College Decision

I was born in Mobile, Alabama, in 1947, and while I was still an infant, my parents moved back to their hometown of Camden, Alabama. My father was a pastor for as long as I can remember, and my mother was a devout woman of Christian faith. We lived in a part of the area known as "The Hills." Although it does not directly impact this particular account, it's important to mention that segregation by race was still strictly enforced. By law, Blacks, or "Coloreds," as we were then known, did not mix with Caucasians, commonly referred to as "White folks" at that time. All of the former Confederate states had laws that regarded people of color as less than fully human and, therefore, not entitled to the dignity, respect, and fundamental freedoms afforded to "normal humans."

Our home, until 1956, was a four-room shack my father inherited from his parents when they passed in the early 1940s. At the time, we had no electricity or running water, known as pressurized water lines. Consequently, it was a regular chore to fetch water from the spring, which was about a quarter-mile down the hill from our house. We had to carry buckets of water up the hill almost daily. When we needed larger quantities of water, especially for washing clothes, Daddy would drive to one of the nearby creeks, fill tubs with water, and bring them back home. This was our main source for doing laundry and other chores.

My mother cooked on an iron stove, which ran on wood. We would cut down trees and dig up stumps, as the stumps made excellent kindling to start the fire. The same stove was also used to heat water for our daily baths. We bathed by heating water and pouring it into a second tub (which held about 2 gallons), then using that to wash ourselves. This was our simple routine for staying clean and managing household tasks.

Our home lacked indoor plumbing, so we relied on "slop jars" to dispose of human waste. Each morning, or as needed, we would throw the waste into the woods adjacent to our house. Our nearest neighbor lived nearly a mile away. We had an "outhouse" about 40 feet behind our home, but it was rarely used because of the unbearable stench, and as is typical with such outhouses, maggots could be seen in the waste below. Often, we would find a log in the woods to dispose of our bodily waste. Such was the overt country life in the hills. Remember that this was the way of life for the entire Black population in the "hill" area of Camden.

I was saved, sanctified, and filled with the Holy Ghost during a revival at my home church, St. John Baptist Church in Camden. Additionally, a note on the educational challenges Black children faced in racially segregated schools: When I was in sixth grade, my teacher, Mrs. C. H. Whorter, recognized my aptitude for math, geometry, and algebra. She challenged one of the high school teachers of 12th-grade algebra and had me visit the 12th-grade algebra class to solve some problems that the seniors were struggling with. That experience solidified my decision to major in

Mathematics when I entered college.

I graduated from Camden Academy High School in May 1964 and applied for entrance to Tuskegee Institute, where I was accepted for the fall semester of that year. However, since my older brother, Sol, wasn't accepted to Tuskegee, my parents decided we should attend the same school. As a result, the decision was made for us both to attend another HBCU (Historically Black College and University), Alabama State University. In the winter of 1965, we enrolled and began attending ASU (which at the time was officially called Alabama State Teachers College).

At the first meeting of my college math class, the instructor explained that the prerequisites were 1st and 2nd high school geometry and 1st and 2nd high school algebra, both of which I had taken. She then mentioned that it was also assumed we had studied trigonometry and calculus. I had never even heard of these branches of mathematics. Later, I discovered that these courses were offered only at "White schools" under the so-called "separate but equal" system.

Students graduating from Camden Academy and other Black schools were limited, not by their ability to learn, but by a curriculum designed by white intellectuals who either didn't understand or didn't care that denying a proper education to "Coloreds," as we were called then, was a disservice to the entire country; the denial of these educational resources held back valuable God-given potential.

Now, let me tell you about the weekend life of four country boys from the rural area of Camden,

Henry Leon McNeil

Alabama. My two brothers and I spent the first nine years of our lives together in a dilapidated house passed down to my parents from my father's father, Deacon John Henry McNeil, who had passed away before my birth in 1947. Our home was about a mile from the nearest neighbor and five miles from the town of Camden. Like most of our neighbors and even our church, St. John Baptist, we had no electricity. Our water source was a spring, about a football field's distance down the hill from our house. The road to town was mostly gravel during my childhood. It was finally paved with slag about two years before we moved in 1956 to a house with electricity, running water, and two indoor bathrooms. I could say much more about my upbringing, but I'll "cut across the cornfield" and get to the part where God interceded for four young men who were enjoying themselves with strong drinks, telling lies, and smoking cigarettes.

In the winter of 1965, I started attending Alabama State College (now Alabama State University) with my older brother, Sol. We both graduated from high school together in May 1964. We were fortunate enough to attend college thanks to my mother, a schoolteacher, and my father, a 100% disabled World War II veteran. His military service connection allowed all three of his children to attend college tuition-free.

Along with my brother Sol, two of our first cousins also joined us at Alabama State. David and F.C., sons of my uncle, Rev. Fortune Williams. David was two or three years older and graduated two years before F.C., Sol, and me in 1964. After graduating high school, David moved to Paterson, New Jersey, where he worked at a factory. With the money he saved from

Henry Leon McNeil

his job, he purchased a 1957 blue Pontiac. This became our go-to vehicle for traveling from bar to bar and wherever else we wanted to go. Having the same basic background and growing up in the same church and neighborhood, we naturally stuck together. Coming from such a rural area, where bars were completely foreign to us, Montgomery felt exciting. For my brother Sol and me, it was our first real experience without adult supervision. We frequently hung out at the local salons, trying to meet girls. We were now "on our own," and as expected, a few mistakes were inevitable.

Suffice it to say, our grades suffered, and there were times we didn't attend class at all, usually because we were recovering from various stages of hangovers caused by the previous night's alcohol overindulgence.

Around mid-April or May, as I recall, wearing a light jacket, Montgomery provided an electric atmosphere for Alabama State College students (later to become Alabama State University). The city had become known as a hub for protests and demonstrations, mainly because, just nine years earlier, Rosa Parks made her famous stand against segregated buses, sparking the Montgomery Bus Boycott. Our parents had warned us not to get directly involved in the various protests and sit-ins aimed at desegregating public institutions, which were still upheld by state law and not actively challenged by the federal government. However, having experienced the injustices of the separate but unequal system firsthand, we felt a duty to participate in the student protests anyway. No, that's not entirely true! The real reason my brother Sol and I participated in the culmination of the Selma-to-Montgomery march, alongside Rev. Dr.

Martin Luther King Jr. was a bit more personal.

Decision to March

One day in March of 1965, after returning to Trenholm Hall from class, my brother casually suggested, "Let's go join the Civil Rights Selma-to-Montgomery march." This march was to culminate in a large open field, where celebrities would perform, leading up to the next day's final march to the State Capitol. I hesitated and reminded him, "We shouldn't go against our parents' orders by participating in these demonstrations."

Don't get me wrong, our parents were sympathetic and fully supported the goals of the march. However, they were also acutely aware of how vicious Southern white folks could be. Their advice to us was, "Let others do the marching. You can support the cause in other ways."

After I voiced my concerns, my brother quickly countered, "But there are going to be plenty of girls at the field." To which I replied, "Let me grab my coat." We spent that night in the field, surrounded by a large crowd, listening to performances by stars like Sammy Davis Jr., Joan Baez, and Harry Belafonte. Other notable figures, such as poet James Baldwin and actors Pernell Roberts and John Saxon, were also present. The "Cause" led by Dr. King was supported both financially and morally by many prominent individuals.

Henry Leon McNeil

One of the major realizations I recognized was that this march reinforced something I had heard all my life. My parents often said that if it weren't for the good and decent white people, Black people (referred to as "Negroes" back then) wouldn't have survived the so-called "Reconstruction" era. Of course, Reconstruction was only a slight improvement from slavery. For example, in those days, if a white man decided to take a Black man's wife, the only recourse for the husband was to flee with his family or stay and face certain death at the hands of the man and his Klan-like-minded folks.

My apologies for veering off track. As I was saying, thousands of people were at the night rally on the eve of the culminating Selma-to-Montgomery march. The field was filled with mostly young people, ages 16 to 22. The next day, my brother was marching with a young lady. I found myself walking down Dexter Avenue, passing Dexter Avenue Baptist Church (where Rev. Dr. Martin Luther King Jr. was pastor) with Betty Crum, who would later become my girlfriend. I remember counting the lines from the front where Dr. King and other distinguished figures marched, arms linked as a sign of unity. We were about 13 or 14 rows back. Honestly, we didn't care about our position in the march; we were just happy to be a part of it. And, by the way, we didn't tell our parents about our participation until long after I had graduated from Alabama State.

Henry Leon McNeil

Deliverance Night

After the march, we returned to campus life and continued having fun, drinking, and always celebrating. During that time, I drank alcohol like a fish drinks water, and I was smoking two packs of cigarettes a day.

One cool spring night, the four of us, David (my first cousin and son of my mother's brother, Uncle Fortune Charles Williams), his brother F.C., Sol, and I decided to go to a bar about two blocks east of campus. It was conveniently located behind a pig's foot sandwich shop, so when you had your fill of liquor, you could stumble over and enjoy a nice country dish to satisfy your hunger.

That night, as usual, we had pooled together our pennies, nickels, and dimes to purchase liquor from the state store before heading to the bar. This was a more economical way to get a buzz than buying all our drinks from the bar. So, there we were around 9 or 10 p.m., sitting at the lounge, drinking beer, and one of us likely had a bottle of "Park and Tilford" whiskey on hand.

Everyone, except my brother Sol, was smoking cigarettes. At this time in my life, I was smoking about two packs a day. This fact will become relevant later in the story.

We were having a great time, telling stories and flirting with the young ladies, as usual. Alcohol can feel like a great experience at the moment, but as I've learned, it can also lead to some of the most horrific situations in a person's life.

Let's move on: we were sitting at the table, drinking in abundance, thinking we were having the time of our lives, when F.C. suddenly got up and wandered off. We didn't think much of it, assuming he had gone to the bathroom.

Little did we know, he wandered off and somehow stumbled upon the most dangerous situation and encountered the three most treacherous individuals in the lounge, or perhaps in the entire city. After F.C. had been away from our table for about 10 or 20 minutes, a burly-looking man approached us just before he returned. His skin was commonly referred to as "blue-black," a description often used for men who had the misfortune of being part of Alabama's notorious prison "Chain Gang." This extreme darkness came from working sunup to sundown in Alabama's scorching heat with no respite. Judging by his appearance, this man looked fresh off the chain gang.

As he approached our table, he complained that our friend, F.C., had come over to his table, where he and two other recently released prisoners were drinking. When I glanced over, sure enough, two other men just as "blue-black" as him were sitting there at his table. The man explained that F.C. had deliberately stepped on his brand-new shoes, which he had just bought after gaining his freedom. He informed us that the three of them had been released from prison that day after serving time for murder, and they were simply trying to enjoy their first night of freedom. He made it clear that they didn't want any trouble but warned us that if F.C. didn't stay away from them, there would be "consequences."

Henry Leon McNeil

When F.C. returned to our table, we told him about the man's visit and his request that F.C. stay away from their table. But, predictably, F.C. became irate, muttering all kinds of expletives about the ex-cons, though thankfully, not loud enough for them to hear.

In hindsight, we should have appreciated the fact that this man had approached us with a certain amount of restraint. His soft tone reminded me of a Bible passage:

Proverbs 15:1-3 (KJV): "A soft answer turneth away wrath: but grievous words stir up anger. The tongue of the wise useth knowledge aright: but the mouth of fools poureth out foolishness. The eyes of the Lord are in every place, beholding the evil and the good."

And so, we continued our indulgence, drinking, smoking, and laughing, when suddenly, the same "blue-black" man returned. This time, his tone was more direct. He explained again that F.C. had deliberately stepped on his shoes and, once more, reiterated that they didn't want trouble but were fully prepared to handle it. He warned us that this was the final warning and there would not be a third.

At that point, we all knew what that meant and tried to warn F.C. about his behavior. But F.C. was acting out of character, undoubtedly due to his drunkenness. However, as we all know, intoxication doesn't excuse bad behavior, especially when it risks harm or discomfort to others. F.C.'s rude behavior, directed without provocation toward the most dangerous and desperate individuals in the room, was inviting disaster. These men were not only ferocious but likely represented the worst that the state of Alabama, or perhaps the entire nation, had to offer.

So, we sat back down, once again trying to enjoy our night. We continued drinking excessively, laughing, and telling stories, as was our usual behavior on such nights out.

Then, it happened, the final episode. We were laughing and enjoying ourselves when, suddenly, the same man came rushing to our table. This time, he wasn't here to talk or give warnings. No, this time, He was making sure that we now understood that he and his friends had decided on reenlisting with the Alabama Department of Corrections.

At that moment, we knew our lives were about to end abruptly, but for God's intervention. By this time, my older brother Sol had already passed out from overindulging in alcohol. The three desperados proceeded to make a statement designed to display their full, satanic potential.

Note: Even though this event took place in 1965, I never stopped long enough to ask any of the three attackers for their names. For clarity, I will assign them names here so you can follow what happens in the series of confrontations that ensue. The very first attack was initiated by the same person who had visited our table twice before, so let's call him Con #1.

Con #1 must have felt entitled to some special privilege, eager to beat up on us "college boys," as he surely felt violated by F.C.'s actions. He rushed over, spewing a loud and boisterous outburst filled with an assortment of curses as if preparing himself psychologically and emotionally for what he thought was about to happen.

Time has a strange way of passing at an almost unimaginable speed when you're faced with a real threat of death and chaos. As Con #1 approached F.C., raising his hand and brandishing a very large Bowie knife, I looked up to Heaven and called on the Master and Author of my faith. Being a young Christian and a true child of God, I knew that He could hear me no matter where I was.

As Con #1 advanced toward F.C. from behind, the other two men dashed toward the door, loudly announcing their intention to go to their car to retrieve weapons of certain destruction.

At that moment, everything seemed to happen in a blur. But the very first thing I did was talk to God. I made a vow: "Lord, if You let us out of this situation without serious injury, I will stop smoking cigarettes."

As soon as I finished my plea to God, Con #1 had the Bowie knife poised just over F.C.'s shoulder. As the knife began to travel downward towards F.C.'s body, God or His Representative turned his knife around so that the butt of the knife struck F.C., causing all of us to scatter. However, I wasn't about to leave my older brother Sol slumped over the table, "drunk as a skunk," as the saying goes. Despite his drunken stupor, I lifted him up and dragged him to David's 1957 Pontiac.

Just as I got Sol into the back seat, Con #2

showed up. As I leaned back out of the car after placing my brother inside, Con #2 struck me across the head with a fierce slap. Without thinking, my reflexes kicked in, and I drew back my fist to defend myself. But as I prepared to engage Con #2, I heard the distinct sound of a pump-action shotgun being cocked. Being from the rural area of Camden, Alabama, I immediately recognized the sound. Con #3 then shouted, "If you lay one hand on Con #2, I'll blow your head off!"

Meanwhile, F.C. was struggling to escape from Con #1, as I wisely decided not to challenge a 12-gauge shotgun. I spun around and ran, leaving half of my brand-new coat, purchased by my mother, in his hand. I was moving so fast that later, one of the young ladies from campus told me she saw me running past her at a speed that rivaled the world-class sprinter Bob Hayes, who was considered the fastest man alive at the time. She said it was a strange sight to see, with half of my coat gone and the other half flapping like a flag in the wind. I was running so fast that I barely had time to think about the fact that I had left my brother Sol in the car. However, I didn't think the attackers would harm a helpless drunk man.

When I finally made it back to my room at Trenholm Hall, I found F.C. and David already there, sitting on the bed and catching their breath. One of them asked, "Where's Sol?" I explained that I had run from the car in a desperate attempt to escape being killed by the attackers and was too terrified to go back. F.C., the one who had started this whole ordeal, volunteered to go back for the car and get Sol. A little while later, he returned, dragging my brother with him.

Henry Leon McNeil

After they arrived, I retrieved two cartons of cigarettes and gave them to either David or F.C., I don't remember which. That night marked the last time I smoked a cigarette. I learned from my parents that when you make a vow to God, you must keep it. And I have kept that sacred vow ever since. I know that by the grace of God, we all eventually made it out of the lounge without serious injury. Even fifty-nine years later, I remain deeply thankful to God Almighty for sparing our lives that night.

That night, I gave praise and thanks to God, my Savior, for saving our lives from those extremely dangerous men. Just as God delivered David from Goliath, He delivered us from harm that night. God heard my plea from the midst of a bar, a place not designed for worshiping the true and living God of Abraham, Isaac, and Jacob. Yet, our story proves that God is omnipresent and able to deliver us from danger, even when our intentions are less than righteous.

In the midst of our spiritual low, God chose not to ignore my cry for help.

One should understand that the bar or the lounge isn't the place that you would normally go to worship, commune, or hear from God. And certainly, such a place isn't where those of us who are Christians go to give reverence to our Lord and Savior Jesus Christ. Nevertheless, this episode teaches us that God is everywhere.

DIVINE DELIVERANCE IN VIETNAM

Avoiding the Draft

Back in 1964, when I graduated from Camden Academy High School, one of the primary concerns for male graduates was finding a plausible way to avoid getting drafted into Uncle Sam's Army, as it was commonly called in those days. Another equally important task was to steer clear of any potential trouble with the overwhelmingly dominant white population. At that time, the idea of Negroes voting was a distant, almost unimaginable reality. As a result, every aspect of government, including the U.S. draft, in our part of the country was controlled and managed by the so-called "powers that be," as Governor George Wallace used to say.

It's absurd that our school system carried the label "separate but equal," as nothing could have been further from the truth. Every facet of Negro life was starkly unequal when compared to that of white people. In those days, whites didn't even bother to hide their blatant acts of entitlement. Questioning the system of white privilege was not only considered bold or reckless; it could be grounds for a lynching.

Now, back to the issue at hand: avoiding the draft. There were several situations that could keep your name off the local draft board's radar. While I don't remember all the deferments available at the time, I do want to highlight something that was well understood. If your parents were wealthy (which automatically excluded 99% of Negroes), you could often have a powerful state or federal official intervene on your behalf, exempting you from military service.

However, there was one type of deferment that was more practical and available even for Negroes: the educational deferment. This option was available to those who could afford to attend college, but it came with certain restrictions, primarily financial. Fortunately for me, my father's veteran disability, rated at 100%, made all of his children eligible for federal assistance to cover most of their college expenses.

The four years of undergraduate college flew by, and before you could say "Joe Louis." I graduated from Alabama State University in January 1969, and soon after, I was recruited by J & L Steel, a Fortune 500 company, to work as a Financial Management Trainee. I accepted the offer and began my career in financial management. However, it was time once again to face the looming threat of the draft. In fact, it was more of a certainty: as soon as you finished your four years of college, your draft status would change from being "exempt" as a student to being "eligible" for service. And once that deferment status was lifted, it wasn't long before you received an order, not an invitation from Uncle Sam, welcoming you to the armed services. In the summer of 1969, I received my unwanted "invitation" from the U.S. Army with orders to report for duty shortly thereafter.

Getting Drafted

In one sense, it was a relief to finally stop having the cloud of the military draft hanging over my head. So, instead of fleeing to Canada like so many others, I reluctantly entered the armed services despite my strong desire to avoid it. Frankly, I wanted nothing more than to avoid the draft, but since my educational deferment had expired, I had no other option.

It was time to end my lease with my roommate, Chris Croom, and make arrangements to sell my new 1968 Grand Prix Pontiac, as well as get rid of other belongings that I wouldn't be taking with me to the military. Interestingly enough, due to the Vietnam War being in full force, the military induction station was passing almost everyone as fit for service, whether they were "crippled, crazy, or blind."

Of course, that's an exaggeration, but the standards for being considered fit for service were extremely low. If you were breathing even a little, you were in.

At that time, my father pastored four churches in Alabama- St. John Baptist on the 1st Sunday and Magnolia Baptist on the 2nd Sunday in Camden. The 3rd Sunday was Rock West Baptist in Canton Bend and Concord Baptist in Concord, Alabama, on the 4th Sunday. Once my family and the circuit of local churches my father pastored were informed of my draft, the prayer wagon was put into motion. Those old saints began intercessory prayer to the God of Abraham, Isaac, and Jacob.

Henry Leon McNeil

Although I was a member of St. John Baptist, I attended all of the churches on their respective Sundays since my father was the pastor. Back then, children didn't have the option of not going to church. My parents never asked me if I wanted to go because I knew that if I wanted to live at home, I had to abide by their rules. Questioning those rules was done at your own peril.

Going off to boot camp was somewhat uneventful because my father had already told me what to expect. He said it would make a man out of a boy, and that certainly became true for me. However, it took time, training, and then some. In any case, I knew that St. John Baptist, my father's other churches, my coworkers at J & L Steel, my fraternity brothers from Alpha Phi Alpha, my family, and everyone who knew me were talking to God Almighty about my situation.

My parents were most worried when they found out I was headed to war in Vietnam. I prayed, too, but my lifestyle at the time wouldn't have been described as "walking in the light," if you know what I mean. This reminds me of the song "My Mother Prayed for Me." The lyrics go: "She had me on her mind, took the time to pray for me. I'm so glad she prayed. I'm so glad she prayed. I'm so glad she prayed for me." That song held true meaning for me because I am indeed grateful that my mother, father, brothers, and all of my family and friends prayed for me.

The series of miracles that spared my physical body from the annihilation that later befell my battalion was a direct result of those prayers. As the Bible says:

Henry Leon McNeil

**James 5:16, "The effectual fervent prayer of
a righteous man availeth much."**

After Joining the Army

While in boot camp (Basic Training), my platoon
leader was a guy named Willis M. Mitchell from
Valdosta, Georgia. I liked being friends with Willis
because he was more mature than most of the other
guys in our platoon. After all, unlike many of these
recent high school graduates, I was older, having
already finished college and been employed at a major
company when I was drafted. Willis also seemed older
and more mature than the others in our group. On
weekends, we often hung out together, telling stories
and drinking whenever we had the chance.

As I mentioned earlier, basic training at Fort
Benning was uneventful. Our company commander
was Captain James H. Kenton, but the person we heard
from most often was Senior Drill Sergeant Kid B.
Cradle. He took great pride in letting everyone know
that he was more than willing to "take off his shirt,"
meaning to match our rank and "kick your behind."
Standing at about 5'2", he constantly challenged every
private in boot camp, no matter their size. His chest
was full of combat medals, and it was said that he had
engaged in hand-to-hand combat with the Vietnamese
and survived. Frankly, I didn't want to mess with him;
the sight of all those medals was enough to convince
me that he knew how to fight. His booming voice made
it clear that he was always ready to give an impromptu
demonstration to anyone foolish enough to challenge
him.

Henry Leon McNeil

After six weeks of basic training at Fort Polk, Louisiana, I, along with some of my comrades, received orders to report to Fort Lewis, Washington, for further training. My training was on a .50-caliber machine gun mounted on an Armored Personnel Carrier (APC). I also doubled as the driver for the company's Black First Sergeant.

I spent about six months at Fort Lewis before receiving orders to ship out to Vietnam. While stationed there, I enjoyed my weekends with fellow soldiers, most of whom were around my age. Some had been in the army for a few years, but many of us spent our free time in the nearby town of Tacoma, Washington, where there were plenty of single women from various nationalities.

One of my buddies and I spent many weekends drinking excessively and having a good time with his pretty Native American girlfriend and her sister. I remember one night, I decided to go to one of our favorite bars by myself. I was having a great time when a nice woman approached me, and we struck up a conversation. One thing led to another, and she invited me back to her home.

Her house was beautiful, well-decorated, and located in an upscale neighborhood. The living room had a skylight, and the lights were turned down low. She even had a large fish tank with what appeared to be a small shark in it. We drank some more, and by morning, she woke me up and took me back to the base. Though I never saw her again, I remember her as a classy, sophisticated, and very pretty lady. I never asked if she was married; I assumed that since she allowed me to come home with her, she was single. Reflecting on the situation later, I realized how reckless it had been. She could have been dangerous, but I thank God for allowing me to survive what could have been a very risky situation. My church, my parents, and other Christians were praying for me, and I'm grateful for that.

Orders for Vietnam & Home Leave

Somewhere around May 1970, I received my orders to deploy to Vietnam. As was customary for soldiers headed to this infamous war zone, I was granted a 31-day leave to spend time with my family and friends before shipping out.

I'm ashamed to admit that I spent very little time with my mother or father during that leave. You see, I was too busy spending all my savings on wine, women, and other indulgences. My home was in Wilcox County, Alabama, which was still a "dry county" at the time.

Now, let me explain what a "dry county" meant in this part of the world. Simply put, in a "dry county," white people could drink whatever kind of alcoholic beverage they wanted without fear of being fined by the local authorities. On the other hand, "Negroes" (as we were called in those days) could get plenty of moonshine and homemade wine, but if the sheriff or one of his deputies caught you drinking or even just under the influence, you were looking at fines and possibly prison time. The "dry county" law simply didn't apply to white folks, just like many other laws.

To be clear, I remember the local constables sitting on the courthouse lawn, drinking beer purchased from the neighboring county. To my knowledge, there were no stores in Wilcox County that actually sold alcohol.

Long story short, as teenagers and young men, we frequently crossed the county line to visit a beer joint in Dallas County, where the county seat was Selma, Alabama. I remember outrunning the sheriff one night after he tried to catch me. (I do believe the TV series *The Dukes of Hazzard* borrowed from some of our local sheriff-dodging routines!)

Anyway, one particular Saturday night, my brother Sol, one of our friends (either Bobby Thompson or John Rease, I can't recall), and I were returning from Dallas County, crossing the "Seven Sister Bridges" that linked it to Wilcox County. We had loaded the trunk with cases of beer and had plenty of wine in our hands. Yes, we drank and drove back then.

As we crossed the first bridge and headed back to Wilcox County, the sheriff spotted us driving in the opposite direction. He quickly turned around, but by the time he did, we were already going 110 miles per hour. After seeing him slow down, we kept our speed up for about three more miles, then cut the headlights and turned onto a local dirt road. We knew the area well, and we managed to turn off without him seeing our taillights.

We watched him speed by at over 100 miles per

Henry Leon McNeil

hour, and I tell you, it was a close call. We waited "in the cut" for a few minutes before getting back on the road and heading to our destination.

That following Monday, Mr. James Hobbs, the principal of Camden Academy High School, called my dad. He said the sheriff had contacted him, warning us to stop crossing the county line to purchase alcohol.

Anyway, I attended various going-away parties before my deployment, and many of the saints from the neighborhood declared they would be praying for my safe return from the Republic of South Vietnam.

Leave Home for Cam Ranh Bay

When my leave was up, I boarded a plane and began my journey to the Republic of South Vietnam. Our first stop was in Alaska, followed by another stop in Hawaii, where we had a three-hour layover before boarding the plane to our final destination, Cam Ranh Bay, South Vietnam. Interestingly enough, as the flight was banking to position us for a safe landing on the beach at Cam Ranh Bay, I looked out the window and saw bombs exploding and thick smoke rising on a hillside a few miles from our landing site.

Our flight landed without incident, and we were quickly ushered to the military receiving station at Cam Ranh Bay. We were introduced to various officers and non-commissioned officers. One of them was Sergeant First Class Resor, who, as it turned out, was the brother of Secretary of the Army Stanley R. Resor. It was odd to see how senior officers took special care to avoid offending him.

We were there to receive our war-zone indoctrination, but in the meantime, we were given the chance to hang out on the beach for a few days before heading inland to engage in what was often referred to as jungle warfare. I remember hanging out with some of the other soldiers who, like me, were preparing to head inland to the front lines. Of course, during our stay, we frequented makeshift clubs and bars. And as is typical during wartime, there were always women around. I must admit to a personal prejudice I hadn't realized before. I didn't find short women attractive. Consequently, I didn't date any local women who seemed to be available to the G.I.s at Cam Ranh Bay.

Nevertheless, we had big fun gambling and drinking beer and other alcoholic beverages. And when I say "big fun," I mean it. We were already on the beach in South Vietnam, and we knew things would only get worse once we moved on to the next step in our processing. The bay was beautiful, the water was blue, and on my last day before boarding a C-1 airplane to head inland, I had a terrifying encounter. While swimming off the beach, two sharks came within two feet of me and circled around. I quickly exited the water and alerted the lifeguards, who cleared the beach. That was a real scare!

Heading Inland to An Khe

Those of us with orders boarded a C-1 airplane,

which took off at an almost 45° angle into the sky. We flew high for about 20 or 30 minutes, heading to a small airstrip just outside the 1st Infantry Headquarters in An Khe, South Vietnam. We were warned that the area was a high-combat zone as we approached. Because of this, we would be landing on an oval-shaped airstrip designed to allow for steep descents and ascents to avoid anti-aircraft gunfire from the enemy.

We landed safely, and I was assigned to an army barracks at the military post in An Khe, which was under attack by enemy forces. On my very first day inside the combat zone, I nearly killed a South Korean (ROK) soldier. He was lying asleep in the hut where I had been assigned, and being new to the combat zone, I hadn't yet learned to distinguish North Vietnamese soldiers (our enemy) from our South Korean allies.

Explosive satchel charges were going off all around the hutches, and this man was lying asleep. I drew my weapon, but a voice inside me said, "Wait." I nudged him with my gun, and when he awoke, he said, "We need to be on guard because we're under attack by the enemy." That's when I realized he wasn't the enemy. Looking back, I feel that soldiers like me should have had some kind of indoctrination to recognize our allies, such as South Korean soldiers, rather than mistaking them for the enemy. At the time, I didn't even know we had South Korean soldiers fighting alongside us.

This was my first day experiencing real combat, and it was terrifying. I had nearly killed an innocent man while the real enemy was out there, throwing satchel charges at random. I later learned that most of the fighting took place outside the An Khe Command Post compound. The bombing subsided after about an hour, and the next morning, I received instructions to join the 3rd Armored Cavalry unit. I was given live ammunition and an M-16 rifle and loaded onto a truck to travel deep into the jungle to join my battalion, company, and platoon.

Heading Further Inland to the Fire Base

Our battalion, consisting of about 2,500 men, was stationed approximately 7 or 8 miles from the main post at An Khe. The battalion commander, whom we referred to as "The Old Man," was a full-bird colonel who traveled mostly by light helicopter, and his office was located two stories underground. During my first four months in the field (the combat zone), I never met or saw him. In the military, orders travel from the top down, and as a Private First Class (PFC), I was at the very bottom of the chain of command.

During my first few weeks in the field, things went mostly uneventful until payday came, and I didn't receive a paycheck. Not getting paid in a combat zone wasn't an immediate problem at first. However, as time went on, and I began to indulge in the usual customs, like buying watered-down alcoholic beverages from local women (whom we called "Momma Son"), I found myself borrowing money from friends to make such purchases.

One day in mid-June 1970, our platoon went on

patrol because there had been signs of enemy presence in the area. Our platoon included one tank at the rear of the column, another tank leading, and about five or six Armored Personnel Carriers (APCs) in between. My job was to operate the 50-caliber machine gun on the APC right behind the lead tank.

At one point, we stopped so some of the men could relieve themselves. Everyone was relaxed for about five minutes, and I climbed into the driver's seat of the lead tank. Then, all of a sudden, we came under enemy fire. In combat, there's no time to go to your assigned station; you operate whatever weapon is immediately available. That meant I was now driving the tank for the very first time. The gunner on the tank shouted instructions as we fired in the direction of the incoming fire. This was terrifying for me. Not only was it my first major firefight, but I was also operating a major piece of military equipment that I had never been specifically trained to use.

The firefight was brief, but it was dusk, and we called in naval firepower from ships stationed 32 miles away. In the rush to bring in adequate firepower, something went wrong. Our Navy ships, firing artillery shells 32 inches in diameter, nearly hit us. Someone had missed giving the ship's gunners the proper coordinates by just a few points, and the shells exploded uncomfortably close to our position. Fortunately, the firefight ended quickly, with no casualties on our side and no evidence of enemy losses.

God saw fit to spare us that day, and I truly believe it was because of the prayers of the righteous as

Henry Leon McNeil

James 5:16 (KJV) says: "The effectual fervent prayer of a righteous man availeth much."

My church, St. John Baptist, my parents, relatives, and all the saints were praying for me, and God heard their prayers. He was watching over us.

After the firefight, I approached my second lieutenant about going to the base camp to resolve the issue of why I hadn't been paid (due to the misspelling of my name). Whenever a lieutenant sends someone to the base camp, it creates a problem with the number of men required to be on duty. Therefore, such passes were only granted on an emergency basis. So, there I was in the combat field, broke and without any money to buy Momma Son's watered-down whiskey.

In another fierce firefight, we were scattered away from our APCs when the enemy started firing on our platoon. We returned fire in the direction of the enemy and killed two soldiers. Some of our men went over to examine the enemy bodies. I heard that someone even took "souvenirs" by cutting off ears or locks of hair. It was unsettling, knowing I was fighting alongside people who seemed to take pleasure in the death of another human being. Thankfully, that firefight ended quickly, just like the others. My church, St. John, my parents, relatives, and saints everywhere were praying, and God heard their prayers by saving us. God, and only God, was watching over us.

There were a few other skirmishes, but the last major one occurred just before I was ordered to leave the jungle and return to the safety of the base camp. This firefight took place around mid-September 1970,

Henry Leon McNeil

when three of our APCs were stationed on small hills about a mile outside the firebase perimeter as lookout posts.

One APC was stationed on the southwest, another on the west, and I was part of a three-man crew stationed on the north APC. It was a clear, hot day, and we decided to relax with a bit of Momma Son's whiskey. The only problem was that, in a war zone, you're supposed to be alert at all times. But there we were, sitting on the APC, some of the men smoking those funny no-name cigarettes also bought from Momma Son.

We had been on the hill for about five hours when, all of a sudden, smoke appeared out of nowhere. Then, another round of smoke came even closer. The flanking APC from the west sped to our rescue, and the other APC started heading our way. That's when we realized we were under mortar attack from the enemy, and we started returning fire. When the enemy saw we weren't alone, they retreated and left us in peace. My church, my parents, relatives, and all the saints were praying, and once again, God heard their prayers and saved us. God, and only God, was keeping watch over us.

Investigating My Missing Paycheck

By the end of September 1970, I had asked my lieutenant five separate times to let me go in and resolve my pay issue. So, I decided to use an internal military tactic that is effective but potentially problematic. I told my lieutenant that if I couldn't go to the administrative office to fix my pay situation soon, I would request to see JAG (Judge Advocate General's Corps). In the military, a soldier has the right to seek redress if they believe it's necessary, and officers are obligated to allow it, provided the reason is valid. Not being paid for the previous four months certainly met the standard for redress. My 2nd Lieutenant assured me that there would be no need to involve JAG and promised I would be on the truck to the 4th Infantry Division's headquarters the next day.

The next morning, I was on the truck heading to the administrative building. There, I spoke with Specialist 4 about getting my pay records straightened out. He asked for my correct name, social security number, unit, and other pertinent information. It turned out that my name had been misspelled, and that was why I hadn't been getting paid. As I sat at his desk, I noticed he was typing in what we called "hunt and peck" style, looking at the keyboard and pecking out one word at a time. I waited patiently, but eventually couldn't help myself and said, "It seems like I should have your job since I can type 70 words per minute, which is much faster than what you're doing." He smiled and kept pecking away. After about an hour of this, in the heat of the non-air-conditioned military hutch, he finally finished my paperwork and informed me that from then on, I would receive my pay in the combat field like everyone else. I was happy with the outcome, but what happened next was even more unexpected.

1st Miracle

I remember it like it was yesterday. I got up from my seat and walked toward the screen door. As I exited, I could still hear the door slam against the frame behind me. About two seconds later, the clerk who had just processed my papers—someone who didn't know me from Adam came out after me and called, "Hey McNeil! Why don't you go see my supervisor?" I responded, "Who's your supervisor?" He replied, "Colonel Ikea." I said, "I'm a PFC. I don't think I want to bother a Colonel about a post-job." A post-job meant working inside the well-protected and highly guarded base camp perimeters rather than being out in the jungle fighting with minimal protection. I added, "Besides, I'm just a Private, and your supervisor is a Colonel." The clerk laughed and said, "What can he do to you? Send you to the field?" That's when I thought to myself: I was already in the worst possible situation; what could be worse? Anyway, because of the clerk's prodding, instead of heading back to the truck that would take me to my firebase, I decided to see Colonel Ikea. His office was right next to the administrative office I had just left.

2nd Miracle

When I walked into the office, a young Japanese-looking gentleman came to the counter and asked if he could help me. I told him I was looking for Colonel Ikea, and he smiled and said, "I am Colonel Ikea." I explained that I was hoping to get a job inside the post-camp. He smiled again and explained that, over the years, both civilians and military personnel had launched complaints about soldiers being pulled

Henry Leon McNeil

from the combat field into the safe haven of a major post camp. Usually, these were the ones with connections to powerful people. After explaining, he smiled once again and said, "I can't help you, soldier." I quickly persisted, saying, "I am an accountant," and his eyes lit up like the 4th of July. He told me to hold on, quickly picked up the phone, and called the Post Commander. He asked, "Commander, Sir, do you still need the accountant you called about this morning?" The commander must have responded in the affirmative because Colonel Ikea sent me directly to the Post Commander.

3rd Miracle

A couple of minutes later, I arrived at the Post Commander's office. I don't remember his name, but I do recall that he was a medium-height man with a serious, gritty look on his face. As soon as he saw me, he began asking me basic questions like, "What kind of degree do you have?" and "What Fortune 500 company did you work for?" These questions were to determine if I was qualified for the job. I answered all his questions to his satisfaction, and he then called the Major in charge of the NCO & Officers' Clubs on post and gave me instructions on how to get to his office.

Now, keep in mind, I hadn't shaved or taken a bath in about two or three weeks, and I hadn't had a haircut in who knows how long. I looked nothing like a college graduate, but I correctly answered all the questions put to me by these gentlemen. All of the officers questioning me were clean-shaven and didn't have the repugnant body odor that I must have had, considering how long it had been since I last washed.

Henry Leon McNeil

When I left the firebase that morning, I had no intention of landing a comfortable, safe job inside one of the most heavily protected headquarters in the world. There was a saying in An Khe: your life was three times as safe on this base as anywhere in the United States, probably because a three-star General was housed there.

When I arrived at the Major's office, he had gathered all his on-staff officers and non-commissioned officers from the administrative cadre of the Post Club system. I immediately got the sense that they were hoping for someone more representative of the old Southern environment they were used to. Growing up in one of the most "racist" counties in the United States, as Dr. Martin Luther King described it, I knew what I was facing. The deep Southern drawls only confirmed it. It was clear to me that my complexion wasn't what they were hoping for in this safe and comfortable position. The outgoing NCO, the Chief Accountant, was a college graduate who had served his year and was within two or three days of heading back stateside. He gave me a series of accounting questions, which I easily answered because they were textbook questions, fresh in my mind from college. Then, some of the other office personnel and the Major asked me additional questions related to accounting and office behavior. The interviews ended, and the Major told me, "Report back to the Post Commander and tell him that if we need you, we'll call your field unit to have you come in." I thanked the Major and his staff for their time and consideration, then walked back to the Post Commander's office.

When I walked in, the Post Commander looked

Henry Leon McNeil

up and asked, "Well, what did the Major tell you, soldier?" I told him the Major had said to report back to my unit and that they would call me if they needed me. At that point, the Post Commander exploded into a tirade of cursing, using words I had never heard before. I was taken aback because, usually, when a senior officer curses out a lower-ranking officer, the protocol is to have the Private step outside. But the Colonel was literally steaming and had turned red in the face.

He told me to have a seat and said, "I'm going to have to give this @#! a piece of my mind!" He grabbed the phone and called the Major, saying something like, "Major, you've been hounding me for two or three weeks, asking me to find a replacement for the man about to leave your staff. You said you wanted someone with a college degree in accounting or business and someone with experience at a Fortune 500 company. Well, this man has everything you said you needed. Now let me tell you something: The General asked us to find a suitable candidate, and you haven't given me one reason why Private McNeil isn't suitable and totally qualified for the position. So here's what I'm going to do: I'll send this soldier back to his unit in the field. But if you call me one more time asking for help to replace your accountant, I'll bust your %$#&^ down to Private. Do you hear me, Major?"

4th Miracle

Then I heard the Major say, "Yes, sir. Send him on down. We'll show him his sleeping quarters, and he can return to his field base to get his things. He'll report for duty tomorrow."

Henry Leon McNeil

Behold the Lamb of God and how He answered prayers from all the saints.

When I returned to the Major's office, I was greeted in a professional manner, and the staff showed me my sleeping quarters. They also took the time to acquaint me with some of the unique protocols, like always having whiskey and beer in the fridge unless we were expecting high-ranking visitors, which was rare.

There were several things I didn't know at the time that caused the Deputy Post Commander to be so outraged. The Major wasn't aware that orders had been cut to move my unit, the 3rd Armored Cavalry, out of the area within the next day or two. There wasn't any time to waste trying to find someone with the "right" color of skin when the qualified candidate was already standing in front of them. Quite frankly, I was surprised by the sudden urgency to get me moved into base camp, as that wasn't my original reason for going there.

BUT NOW LET ME EXPLAIN HOW THIS ALL BECAME A REAL MIRACULOUS ACT OF GOD.

Just remember that I began requesting permission from my platoon leader to go to the HQ to straighten out my pay since the first payday I missed. I didn't receive a paycheck or whatever form of currency the U.S. military was using at that time in that particular war zone. (I don't recall exactly what type of currency we were using.) I arrived in the area around July 1970 and kept getting the runaround whenever I asked to go to the base camp to resolve my pay issue. I wasn't allowed to go in July or August, and now it was the latter part of September, and I was finally allowed to go in—just two days before my battalion (some 2,500 soldiers) received orders to move into Laos, where they were subsequently massacred.

Special Note: We soldiers were told that the military would never announce or admit to the public that any unit had been massacred, as it would be demoralizing.

Now, if I had been allowed to go to base camp weeks before the battalion orders were written for my unit to ship out to Laos, there wouldn't have been an urgency on the part of the Deputy Post Commander. As a result, the Major could have used his discriminatory tactics to secure a "qualified replacement" for the outgoing accountant. But because I was delayed in going to base camp, God intervened, and everything lined up perfectly.

After returning to the Deputy Post Commander's office, he asked me again, "How did it go?" I explained that they had shown me my living quarters, and everything went fine. He smiled, we exchanged appropriate closing remarks, and that was that.

Back to the Combat Field

I then got on the vehicle that took me and the others back to the battalion firebase, which marked the beginning of a very unsettling set of circumstances.

Henry Leon McNeil

5th Miracle

As I approached my APC, waiting for me was a 1st Lieutenant. There were several causes for concern here.

1. My immediate leader was a 2nd Lieutenant, a rank lower than a 1st Lieutenant.
2. In a war zone, when an officer of a higher rank is waiting for a private, it can only mean serious trouble.

To top it off, the 1st Lieutenant started by asking, "Are you Private Henry L. McNeil?" I responded, "Yes, sir."Then he said, "The Old Man ordered me to wait by your track (armored personnel carrier) until you returned from base camp."I asked if he knew why the Colonel wanted to see me. He replied, "I don't know, soldier, but I'm glad I'm not in your shoes right now." Disturbing thoughts immediately ran through my mind:

A. In a combat area, a field commander like our Full-Bird Colonel could issue a summary execution for offenses like falling asleep on guard duty, which could endanger the entire battalion.

B. As the 1st Lieutenant escorted me to the elevator that would take me two stories underground to see the Colonel, he said, "Bear in mind, PFCs don't go to the Old Man's office. Most of us never even see him." Then he added, "Soldier, I wouldn't want to be in your shoes right now."

Henry Leon McNeil

When I saw the Colonel, I immediately saluted him. He told me to be "at ease," and right away, he could see that I was scared stiff. Sensing my fear, he quickly said, "Please don't be afraid, I only called you down here to inquire about some extremely unusual happenings today." He began his inquiry by saying, "I called your platoon commander in to ask why you had been sent to Headquarters, and he assured me that it was to resolve your pay issue." I confirmed, "Yes, sir, the Lieutenant is correct. I was sent to Base Camp to straighten out my pay."The Colonel then asked, "Did they resolve your pay situation, soldier?"I replied, "Yes, sir."Satisfied with my response, he then said, "Now, I want to ask you just a few important questions..."

Orders to Come Out of Combat

When we arrived at the Colonel's office, there were several other ranking officers waiting for me. My knees were knocking as I walked in. Apparently, they all wanted to hear the explanation of how a private had orders cut within the same hour as the command was given—and how those orders were flown by helicopter from Headquarters in An Khe to our firebase. Majors, 1st and 2nd Lieutenants were all ears, while my fellow soldiers (the enlisted men above ground) didn't understand what all the fuss was about.

The Colonel began, "Are you related to Senator Brooks of Massachusetts?" I responded that I was not related to him. (Senator Edward Brooke was the only

Black U.S. Senator at the time.) Seeing the

bewilderment on my face, the Colonel didn't immediately explain why he had asked the question.

Then he looked me in the eye and asked, "Who are you, soldier?"I replied, "I am Private Henry L. McNeil."

He said, "Let me explain why I'm asking these questions. Recently, Congress passed legislation that prohibited soldiers in combat from using their ' at-home' influence to get out of the field and into a safe assignment at a major headquarters. This was meant to prevent preferential treatment for the sons of the rich and powerful. Once you were in the combat field, you were expected to stay there until your term of service ended, and you were sent back stateside. But something very strange is going on, and I'm trying to get to the bottom of it." Then he continued, "About a half-hour before the truck you were on returned from Headquarters, a helicopter flew in from HQ carrying nothing but your orders. Everybody knows that helicopter fuel is expensive, and we don't use a warrant officer's time to fly a private's orders 'all willy-nilly." He paused, then added, "Notwithstanding the fact that the orders were signed by a three-star General." Once again, he asked, "Who are you, soldier?" This time, I replied, "I am a child of God."

The Colonel nodded and said, "I've been in the army for more than 15 years, and I've never seen a private's orders flown anywhere exclusively. Not only that, but I'm a Full Bird Colonel, and my orders are signed by a Brigadier General (one star), while yours are signed by a Lieutenant General (three stars). Furthermore, it usually takes between 1½ to 2 weeks for a decision to be made and orders to be delivered to a soldier. But in your case, the orders were cut within the same hour and flown out the same day." He then asked, "What kind of education do you have, soldier?"

I explained that I had a degree in business administration from Alabama State University. The Colonel looked at me with surprise and said, "According to your Battalion Firebase records, the highest education you attained was finishing eighth grade." I explained that I had understated my education while in the combat field to avoid potential jealousy or issues with the soldiers I was serving with. He nodded in understanding. As I had mentioned before, the Major and even the Colonel didn't have high enough clearance to know that orders had been cut to move the 3rd Armored Cavalry out of the area within a day or two. The Colonel didn't need to know that information, but from the strange circumstances, he knew the Generals were up to something, even if he didn't know exactly what, when, or where. I must admit that when I was first summoned to this meeting, I was terrified about why I had been called before "the Old Man." However, by the end of the meeting, it seemed like the Colonel was more worried than I was.

That night, I was assigned to guard duty, which meant going out about a football field's distance from the firebase to watch for any possible enemy activity. It was the first time I had been on guard duty since arriving at the firebase. The night passed uneventfully, and early the next morning, I got on a truck with all of my belongings and headed to my new assignment with the NCO & Officers Club system at the Headquarters Post in An Khe, South Vietnam.

Henry Leon McNeil

James 5:16 (KJV): "Confess your faults one to another, and pray one for another, that ye may be healed. The effectual fervent prayer of a righteous man availeth much."

Let's face it, I would have never made it out of the combat field but for the prayers of the righteous. We need to understand that even while we are wallowing in our iniquity, the prayers of the righteous, those who have dedicated themselves to the cause of Jesus Christ, are heard. The Lord hears and answers the prayers of the righteous, even when those being prayed for can't get through because of their own sins. Prayer is so necessary for many reasons, but one that stands out is the closeness it brings to God. There's no other way to achieve that kind of connection. Prayer is an extremely effective medium through which we have access to Almighty God.

At HQ in An Khe

Being in charge of approximately 16 NCO clubs and assisting with the Officers' clubs was quite a responsibility. However, it was a much better and safer position than serving as a .50-caliber machine gunner on an armored personnel carrier. I was thankful to the Lord God Almighty for answering the prayers of the righteous. This was especially true when you consider that on the same day, I was transferred to the safe haven of the 4th Infantry Division Headquarters in An Khe, my former battalion received orders to invade Laos. They were actually moving in that direction as I was settling in at An Khe. The angels in heaven were surely watching over me.

Those who have experienced combat know that the military almost never reveals or admits when a substantial unit is overrun or massacred. However, troops in a combat zone have their own ways of communicating such tragedies, despite the military's code of silence meant to keep soldiers and civilians from being demoralized by battlefield atrocities. Word came through the ranks that my battalion was utterly destroyed during the invasion of Laos, with reportedly no survivors.

Now that I was inside one of the most protected military posts on earth, I settled in and began having regular update meetings with my Major and the General, who was the post commander. Keeping the books and ensuring that proper accounting procedures were followed became my daily task. I worked with a nice group of soldiers, and I stayed in this position for about four months before the 4th Infantry Division received some bad news—or at least, I thought it was bad news for me.

When I first came to Vietnam, I had a combat MOS (Military Occupational Specialty) code of 11D. In the military, even when you're assigned a different type of job, sometimes you retain your original MOS. This wasn't good for me because although the 4th Infantry was leaving to go back stateside, I still had about five or six months to go before my tour was up, which meant I couldn't ETS (End Term of Service) back to the USA.

Naturally, I was worried stiff that I would be sent back to the battlefield. I asked one of my buddies about my status, and he told me I would most definitely be sent back to the field since my record still listed me as a .50-caliber machine gunner. Thank God for Jesus' prayers kept going up for me back home, and the angels in heaven were still watching over me. Someway, somehow (I still don't know who), someone changed my combat MOS to an office-type MOS, and I was sent to Long Binh in the Saigon area, another large and relatively safe post camp in South Vietnam. Once again, the angels in heaven were watching over me.

At the time, I was keeping a diary that recorded the names of those serving with me and the events of each day. However, when I was preparing to ship out to Long Binh, a "lifer" (those who would retire from the military) told me that if I wanted to see my belongings again, I shouldn't put them on the Army trucks for transport. He explained that the Army routinely lost soldiers' personal items during these transfers. Unfortunately, I didn't listen, and sure enough, I never saw my personal items again. As a result, I'm writing this without the names of the soldiers I served with 50 years ago. I later learned that the Army's Intelligence Unit regularly reviewed personal items for any written accounts to weed out spies and other threats.

From An Khe to Long Binh, South Vietnam

When I arrived at Long Binh, I quickly realized that this camp was much larger than the one I had just left. By this time, I had been in Vietnam for more than eight months, and the local women were starting to look beautiful to me, regardless of their height.

Henry Leon McNeil

My work consisted of routine accounting and conducting surprise audits of the NCO and Officers' clubs. At this facility, I was no longer the Chief Accountant but rather one of the accountants reporting to a small hierarchy that included a Captain, a 1st Lieutenant, and a very powerful Sergeant Major named Perez. The job was mostly uneventful until I went on a week's leave, spending three days in Saigon and four days in Bangkok, Thailand. Needless to say, I had a ball in both places.

In Saigon, my friends and I found a soul food restaurant that sold collard greens, pig's feet, cornbread, chitterlings, and more. There was plenty of wine, women, and songs. Oddly enough, when I got to Bangkok, I met a beautiful Black woman who stayed with me the entire three days, even though she could barely speak a word of English. She was tall, Black, and very pretty.

A guy I met in Saigon traveled with me to Bangkok, and he fell in love, deciding to marry his girlfriend there. We had a great time together. After I returned stateside the following year, I was on an audit assignment in Detroit, Michigan, in 1972. The friend who married the girl from Bangkok was still in Vietnam, but he had asked me to visit his wife whenever I was in Detroit, which was his hometown. I did visit her briefly, as she was living with his parents at the time. I met the family, we talked for a bit, and that was the last time I saw them.

Anyway, I took one more leave and spent a week in Sydney, Australia. What a wonderful place to party with girls, girls, and more girls! There's a lot I could share about my stay in Sydney, but that's not what this writing is about.

In July of 1971, I boarded a plane in Saigon and headed back to the USA. By the grace and mercy of God, in response to the prayers of my church (St. John), my parents, relatives, and saints all over, God heard and answered those prayers and allowed me to come home safely. To God be the glory, honor, and praise.

I remember buying my mother a small present while waiting at the airport in Saigon. It was a simple, inexpensive ring with a stone in it. When I returned home and gave it to her, you would have thought I had given her the crown jewels! She made such a fuss about the gift her son brought back from Vietnam. Honestly, I felt bad that I hadn't taken the time or spent more money to buy her a better gift. However, the way she reacted made it clear that it wasn't about the material value; it was about the love and thought behind the gesture. She was overjoyed that I remembered to bring her something from Vietnam. Both my parents were thrilled to see me return home safely. Many families were not so fortunate. When I left for Vietnam a year earlier, I didn't think I had much of a future. When I came back, I had to start over, with one exception: the government required companies to hold the jobs of veterans while they were away at war. I didn't have a car, and I found an uncashed check I had left in my old bedroom drawer. In any case, I was extremely glad to be home again and out of the war zone. Of course, I was also excited to see the positive changes that had taken place in local government during the one year I was gone.

Henry Leon McNeil

When I returned home, I noticed some interesting changes. For example, the office personnel were no longer using mechanical calculators; they were using digital technology, which hadn't been available when I left the corporate world to serve in Vietnam. Also, when I left in 1970, Black people couldn't vote in Wilcox County, Alabama. The entire local government was controlled by White people. This was painfully obvious when I had to visit the county courthouse before leaving for Vietnam. Every person working there was White. But when I returned in 1971, the majority of courthouse employees were Black. It was a very encouraging change and a powerful reminder of how important the voting process is when done fairly.

Divine Deliverance from Stage 4 Cancer in 1998

If God were to treat us as our sins deserve, we wouldn't have a chance to see the Kingdom of God. But when we read Psalm 103, we find that God deals with us through compassion and grace (verse 8), not by holding His anger against us continuously (verse 9). Let's take a brief look at Psalm 103:

103:2-4: Bless the Lord, O my soul, and forget not all his benefits: 3 Who forgiveth all thine iniquities; who healeth all thy diseases; 4 Who redeemeth thy life from destruction; who crowneth thee with lovingkindness and tender mercies;

Henry Leon McNeil

11-15: For as the heaven is high above the earth, so great is his mercy toward them that fear him.12 As far as the east is from the west, so far hath he removed our transgressions from us.13 Like as a father pitieth his children, so the LORD pitieth them that fear him.14 For he knoweth our frame; he remembereth that we are dust.15 As for man, his days are as grass: as a flower of the field, so he flourisheth. 16 For the wind passeth over it, and it is gone; and the place thereof shall know it no more.

- **Verse 2** speaks to the benefits of being connected to God.
- **Verse 3** reminds us that God forgives our sins and heals all our diseases.
- **Verse 4** speaks of God's redemptive power, reaching down from heaven to take us out of the pit of destruction and crown us with love and compassion. Oh, what a mighty God we serve!
- **Verses 11, 12, 14, and 15**, respectively, tell us that God grants mercy and removes our sins as far as the East is from the West. He remembers that we are dust, describing our life as grass, flourishing like a flower, and then, with the wind, it is gone. But God's love is from everlasting to everlasting for those who fear Him, and His righteousness extends to their children and grandchildren, to those who keep His covenant and obey His precepts.

Henry Leon McNeil

Let me explain what I believe was the physical reason for my body being in such bad shape. To be real, I drank heavily during high school, always undercover moonshine and homemade drinks since our county was dry, meaning no alcoholic beverages were sold. I continued to drink heavily in college at Alabama State, from which I graduated in January 1969. After graduation, I was recruited by J & L Steel Corp., which later became LTV Steel. After work, I would almost always stop at a favorite local saloon and drink more alcohol than anyone should.

Back then, the police didn't deal harshly with drunk drivers. On at least two occasions when I was caught drunk driving, the police simply escorted me home instead of arresting me. I drank heavily right up until the moment I accepted God's call on my life on Saturday, December 24, 1988. It was an interesting day, to say the least. I had planned to get drunk on Christmas Eve, but God, in His grace, mercy, and infinite wisdom, changed the course of my entire day. I remember going to the liquor store and spending $84 on alcohol, waiting in line to make my purchases. I headed home around noon, unloaded the liquor onto the table, and then, right in front of my wife, I announced that I was going to acknowledge my call to the preaching ministry by informing my pastor, Rev. W.C. Bunton. My wife, Leslie, thought I was "off my rocker," as the scene must have been confusing at best.

Anyway, I called Pastor Bunton on the phone. Even though it was Saturday (a day he usually didn't work), he answered my call. I informed him that God had called me to the preaching ministry, and he responded that my call was an answer to his prayers for help at Shiloh Baptist Church in Canton. He had been praying diligently for help because two of his assistants were in their 90s and suffering from health issues, and the third was in his 40s, but the church had around 350 members, so he needed more assistance.

Before I move on, let me explain something about God's call, whether it's a call to preach, sing, heal, or any other ministry. Many people ask:

1.   How do I know I was called?
2.   Why did I accept the call at such an unusual moment?

These are relevant questions, especially considering the event of December 24, 1988, when I was loaded down with bags of alcohol and had no intention of answering any call. My answer to both questions is simple: The Creator never had difficulty communicating a thought, message, or action to any of His creations. You might resist, like I did, and the outcome may be different for you; you might not live to talk about it.

It's simple: God let me know He had had enough of my putting off His call for me to preach and minister His Holy Word. He made it clear, as I set down the liquor bags on the table, that if I didn't answer His call, He might just take me home to Him. As my sister, Rev. Dr. Mary Joyner, often said, "God might just decide to take you home with Him if He can't find a reason to keep you down here." Let me be clear: God didn't force me to answer the call, but He made it known that if I didn't, there wouldn't be many more chances. I would be putting on the long white robe in heaven since I didn't seem willing to fulfill His mission for me down here. Let me help you understand: **"God ain't nobody to play around with!"** As Psalm 106:43-44 shows, even though we rebel and sin against God, He is so loving and gracious that He remembers His covenant with our forefathers Abraham, Isaac, and Jacob and often refrains from punishing us as we deserve, instead showing mercy because we are the seed of Abraham (Galatians 3:7).

After answering God's call to preach His Living Word, Pastor Bunton got me involved in various assignments. Soon, I asked the pastor if it would be alright for me to go to seminary, as I could afford the expense at the time. He advised me to wait at least a year to get "rooted and grounded" in the church before pursuing seminary education. I later realized he was right. I needed that grounding immediately after entering the preaching ministry. When you attend seminary, you must be firmly rooted in your beliefs, or an atheistic instructor could cause you to stray from your spiritual foundation. After being under Pastor Bunton's tutelage for about a year, I enrolled in Ashland Theological Seminary, taking about two graduate courses each quarter. Long story short: after serving as an associate of Pastor Bunton for about eight years, one of my closest friends and colleagues at LTV Steel in Akron, Ohio, Pastor Joe Anderson, gave my name and contact information to Mt. Olive Missionary Baptist Church in Dennison, Ohio. After the usual vetting process, I was elected as their pastor in July 1996. This was my first role as the leader of one of God's churches.

Visit to My Pittsburgh Doctor

Henry Leon McNeil

In the summer of 1996, or thereabouts, I visited my doctor in East Liberty, Pittsburgh, because I had noticed some blood in my stool, even though I wasn't experiencing any pain at the time. The doctor examined me, and after I informed him about the blood, he recommended that I undergo a colonoscopy. Since I had never heard of this procedure before, I asked him to explain what it entailed. After he explained, I immediately told him I wouldn't be getting examined that way. Bear in mind, I had never been hospitalized before and had no significant health issues at the time.

The doctor tried to convince me that the procedure was virtually painless and that, thanks to the anesthesia, I wouldn't feel much of anything. Still, I refused. I returned to my home in Akron, not feeling particularly bad until around August 1997, when I started experiencing severe stomach pains. I didn't think much of it at first, as I had always suffered from some degree of gas in my digestive system. But as time passed, the pain progressively worsened, so I went to see another doctor. After an examination, he couldn't find any issues in my upper digestive system but gave me a prescription for gas relief. Unfortunately, the problem didn't improve. In fact, it continued to worsen.

Month by month, week by week, the stomach pains increased. I was living off a bowl of soup a day and, when my digestive system allowed, a hot dog. By November 1997, my weight had dropped from 235 pounds to 185 pounds, and I wasn't trying to lose weight. (For context, I'm 6 feet 2 inches tall.) Because of the weight loss, I no longer needed my diabetes medication in such large doses. I remember seeing a photo of myself from that time, and I looked about 30 years older than I actually was. The stomach pains were so severe that I could barely eat half of a hot dog, and it took five hours for my digestive system to process it.

One night in November, Pastor Bunton, his wife Barbara, Rev. Phillip Stevens, my wife Leslie, and I went to an event at an elaborate country club in Massillon Township. At the event, I pretended to enjoy myself, sipping tiny amounts of soft drinks. However, I became so sick that I had to rush to the restroom to throw up. Afterward, the group decided we should leave. I apologized for ruining everyone's evening, but by that point, I couldn't help how I felt.

How I Was Finally Diagnosed

By the end of November 1997, the pain had become almost unbearable. I scheduled an appointment with my family doctor, but he couldn't determine the problem. He decided to refer me to a specialist, Dr. Bandi. Dr. Bandi thoroughly examined me but was also unable to pinpoint the issue. It was then that I remembered passing blood in my stool back in 1996 and told him about the colonoscopy I had refused to undergo. Upon hearing this, Dr. Bandi immediately ordered a CT scan, which was performed on January 26, 1998, followed by a colonoscopy on February 3, 1998.

A day or two after the procedures, we called the doctor's office for the results. In the meantime, my church (Mt. Olive Missionary Baptist Church in Dennison, Ohio) turned out in great numbers at the hospital, about 24 members came to show their love and support. I was also fortunate to have one of our church members working as a nurse supervisor at the hospital, which certainly helped improve my favor with the nursing staff once they learned I was their boss's pastor.

On February 9, 1998, I had an appointment with Dr. Jones to discuss an upcoming operation to remove a tumor from my colon, not yet knowing if the tumor was cancerous. The purpose of the meeting was to set up the operation and make the necessary arrangements. However, by Friday, the 13th, I insisted on knowing the results of the biopsy and other tests. When we called, the nurse/assistant said the doctor would have to deliver the results himself. From that response, we suspected the news was bad.

My response to this impending bad news was to begin praying for deliverance, first, as mentioned earlier, requesting that any and all satanic obstacles be removed. Second, I acknowledged Romans 3:23 (KJV), "For all have sinned and come short of the glory of God," and realized that I didn't deserve deliverance because of my sins. Romans 6:23 (KJV) says, "For the wages of sin is death, but the gift of God is eternal life through Jesus Christ our Lord." Since I was a part of Jesus' holy and righteous family, I sought His mercy and grace. For the next few hours, I had a very personal conversation with the Master of the Universe, and during this prayer, I found comfort in reading many soothing verses from the Psalms. I prayed sincerely, for one thing I know is that "you can't pull the wool over

God's eyes." It's prudent to be honest and direct with God.

We need to understand that God knows everything about our situation. However, the free will He gave us allows us to make choices when dealing with situations that need the attention of our Lord and Savior, Jesus Christ. But let me help you: your approach to **"the Lily of the Valley, the Bright and Morning Star, Alpha and Omega, the Beginning and the End, the I AM"** should always be honest and upfront. God already knew about your circumstances before the earth was formed. He not only knows what has happened, but He also knows what is happening and what will happen. So do yourself a favor; don't try to lie to God; He is omniscient and knows everything. There's no use trying to hide things from Him.

That Friday, around 4:00 PM, we placed a final call to Dr. Bandi's office, and the nurse said he was seeing another patient. She told us we could come in on Monday for the results. Well, we hung up and rushed over to Dr. Bandi's office, insisting on seeing him that Friday. Dr. Bandi graciously met with us and explained that the reason he hadn't wanted to speak to us that day was that the news was so devastating, he hoped we could enjoy our weekend before hearing it. He revealed that the tests had shown I had colon cancer. He went on to explain that, specifically, after reviewing the CT scan and colonoscopy results, I had a very large tumor, about 3-4 cm in size. Worse, I had Stage 4 colon cancer, meaning the cancer had spread beyond the colon wall and infected other major organs in my body. There was no way to contain or slow the spread. He told me there was no hope for a cure and that I probably had about six months to live. He advised me to get my affairs in order.

God bless her heart, my wife, Leslie, began to cry. The doctor then said he would call one of the leading surgeons in Akron to perform the surgery, Dr. Brian Jones. Dr. Jones reviewed the test results and came to the same conclusion as Dr. Bandi. At some point, I don't recall exactly when, Dr. Bandi had my wife and me focus on a screen that showed an "infrared" image of my vital organs. According to the doctor, almost all of my major organs were infected with cancer. He reiterated that there was no hope of healing and said I would probably be dead within six to seven months.

The Midnight Prayer & Supplication

That Friday night, after receiving the devastating news, my wife and I went home, feeling sadness in one sense, but I had the hope of Jesus Christ living inside of me. I knew that **"It ain't over until God says it's over."** My wife, daughter, and I went to bed at the usual time that night. Around 1:00 AM, the devil woke me up. You may ask, **"How do you know it was the devil?"** If you pay close attention to the thoughts he plants in your mind, you will always be able to distinguish satanic conversation from righteous conversation. The devil said, **"Look at you now! Look what your God has done to you! He waited until you became pastor of a church, and now, in the middle of your ministry, you're stricken with the incurable disease of colon cancer. Look at you,**

you're about to die! Where is your God now?"

After hearing that, I got out of bed and went downstairs into the family room without disturbing my wife. When I arrived in the family room, I immediately fell to my knees and began praying. I started by asking God to remove any satanic influence from me so I could communicate with Him without interference from the devil. And as expected, that's exactly what God did. There was no further satanic influence during my time of prayer. For the next four to five hours, I prayed and communicated with God, reading from His sacred scriptures, especially the Psalms. During that time, I reflected on how many biblical patriarchs had faced what seemed like certain death.

The more I prayed, the more confident I became that I was on the right path to recovery despite the terrible news from the doctor. He had said I had only six months to live, possibly less. I thought about the story of Shadrach, Meshach, and Abednego, who faced a life-threatening situation when they refused to worship King Nebuchadnezzar's golden image (Daniel 3). In verse 15, listen to what King Nebuchadnezzar said to these three Hebrew boys:

Daniel 3:15 (KJV) [15]Now if ye be ready that at what time ye hear the sound of the cornet, flute, harp, sackbut, psaltery, and dulcimer, and all kinds of music, ye fall down and worship the image which I have made; *well*: but if ye worship not, ye shall be cast the same hour into the midst of a burning fiery furnace; and who *is* that God that shall deliver you out of my hands?

Henry Leon McNeil

In verses 16-18, hear the response from these God-fearing Hebrew boys:

Daniel 3:16-18 (KJV) [16]Shadrach, Meshach, and Abednego answered and said to the king, O Nebuchadnezzar, we are not careful to answer thee in this matter. [17]If it be so, our God whom we serve is able to deliver us from the burning fiery furnace, and he will deliver us out of thine hand, O king. [18]But if not, be it known unto thee, O king, that we will not serve thy gods, nor worship the golden image which thou hast set up.

The king ordered them into a fiery furnace, but they trusted in God's power to deliver them, whether He chose to save them or not. Their faith was unconditional, and they knew that even if they died, they would be with God.

These servants of the Most High True and Living God was letting the King know that they valued following the God of Abraham, Issac, and Jacob more than they valued their own lives. When the Hebrew boys requested help from God, notice that they didn't put the condition of deliverance in the request. There are several reasons why you need not make these types of conditions on this type of request. I will name just a few:

1. They didn't know, or would you have known, if God wanted them to experience death at this time or not. In other words: We will serve and honor you unconditionally.

Henry Leon McNeil

2. Since they were only humans, they didn't know how God wanted to use this particular situation or how it would fit into His divine order.

3. Since they were worshippers of the Most High God, they knew that if they died, they would arrive as Abraham did (Luke 16:22) in Heaven, consequently, the fear of death is not present because of their devout belief in the God of Abraham, Isaiah, and Jacob although we can be certain that they didn't want to die in this way and at this particular time since they, no doubt, saw this situation as one of a developing trail/testimony and they were certain as I was that God had never nor will He ever lose ground in such spiritual warfare because He is omnificent, having unlimited creative power. No one can lose when God is fighting for them.

My prayer and supplication to God lasted until about 5 AM. At the end of this worship & devotion, I was confident and knew that God had heard my prayer. Now understand this: When I got up off my knees, I really didn't know if the Lord had determined to let me live here on earth or take me home with Him. The only thing that I was sure of was that God had heard my cry. You see, I didn't approach God with an "attitude of entitlement" lest I misunderstood the scripture found in **Romans 3:23-24 (KJV) [23]For all have sinned and come short of the glory of God**.

I knew that I had no special sort of pass on sin; however, I also knew that God is sovereign and was full of grace and mercy, and when we approach Him in honesty, meekness, confessing our sins and asking for forgiveness, He will give ear to those who are called, for the scriptures say:

Romans 8:28 (KJV) [28]And we know that all things work together for good to them that love God, to them who are called according to *His* purpose.

In the same way, I knew that my God, the God of Abraham, Isaac, and Jacob, could rescue me from this terminal illness, but I also didn't know if He would. After spending about four hours in prayer and meditation, I rose from my knees and felt movement in my stomach. It wasn't discomforting; it was more like a soothing movement, as though something was happening inside me.

As I later reflected, I believe that God was enacting the healing process in my body right after that early Saturday morning spiritual devotion. My God is an awesome God. After my talk with the Creator and Maker of the Universe, I was no longer afraid of dying. Don't misunderstand me, I didn't want to die at that point, but I had reached the same point that Jesus expressed in **Luke 22:42 (KJV): "Father, if thou be willing, remove this cup from me: nevertheless, not my will, but thine, be done."**

There are moments in our Christian walk where we must deliberately and vividly surrender our individual and sometimes selfish will to our Master's

Henry Leon McNeil

divine will. With this gesture, we demonstrate to our Lord and Savior that we have trust and abiding faith in Him. We accept His will for us, even when it involves our very lives. With true Christian faith, we are able to value our Lord's decisions as infinitely more important than our own.

The Doctor's Pre-Op Disclaimer

It was now Monday, after receiving the extremely bad news, and I was at Dr. Brian Jones' office. Dr. Jones spoke to me in a very frank and sober manner. We had both seen a large screen display of the places in my body where cancer had been detected. It was clear that the cancer had spread to many areas, and Dr. Jones echoed Dr. Bandi's sentiments, stating that there was no known effective treatment for the cancer that had infected most of my vital organs. Dr. Jones said, "I am going to remove the 4-cm tumor from your colon, but I have to be honest with you; removing the tumor will not save your life because the cancer has spread beyond the walls of your colon and infected many of your vital organs. Removing the tumor may prolong your life by a few months, but probably no more than six or seven." Then he added, "I will do one thing for you that will do more for your healing than any drug or procedure we have in this or any other hospital. I will pray for your healing." It was comforting to know that I was going to be operated on by a Christian doctor. The surgery was scheduled for February 17, 1998, at Akron City Hospital. I was to be there at 11:00 AM for preparation, with surgery to begin at 1:00 PM.

Henry Leon McNeil

When I arrived at the hospital's waiting room, many of my church members from Mt. Olive Missionary Baptist Church, where I was pastor, were present. Everyone knew by now that I had been diagnosed with stage 4 cancer, and there had been much prayer sent up to heaven on my behalf, for which I am forever grateful.

I want to emphasize one thing here: before this day, I had called every relative, distant and close, and many friends, asking for prayer. I believed in **James 5:16 (KJV): "Confess your faults one to another, and pray one for another, that ye may be healed. The effectual fervent prayer of a righteous man availeth much."**

This scripture assured me that the prayers of the righteous concerning your situation truly matter. All praise be to our Triune God. Remember, whatever battle or obstacle you face today, it is not new. God's people have faced insurmountable battles since the days of the Old Testament. Think of **1 Samuel 17**, when young David volunteered to face the 9½-foot giant, Goliath, in battle. Before King Saul allowed him to fight, David recounted how the Lord had delivered him from both a lion and a bear while he was tending his father's sheep. David declared to Saul that Goliath would face not a small boy but one who fought in the name of the Lord. David said to the Philistine,

1 Samuel 17:45: "Thou comest to me with a sword, and with a spear, and with a shield: but I come to thee in the name of the Lord of hosts, the God of the armies of Israel, whom thou hast defied."

Henry Leon McNeil

In the same way, the battle I was fighting was not merely against cancer; it was against Satan and his forces. On my side was the God of Abraham, Isaac, and Jacob. When the Lord took charge of the battle, Satan was already defeated, though he didn't realize it. The battle had to play out so that God would get full glory, just as David's victory over Goliath demonstrated God's power and strength.

Dr. Jones operated on me starting at 1:00 PM on Tuesday, February 17, 1998, and the operation lasted about five or six hours. Afterward, he came to the waiting room to speak with my wife, Leslie. There were about 25-30 members of Mt. Olive Baptist Church in the waiting room, showing their support. Dr. Jones directed Leslie to a smaller room for a private conversation.

She recounted the conversation with him as follows: "Mrs. McNeil, I have been performing these types of operations for years. I've seen many outcomes and results, but in all my years, I have never seen a case where the body was so full of cancer one week, and then, the following week, there appears to be no cancer. However, I will send a sample of your husband's lymph nodes to an oncologist for further examination."

At 9:00 AM on March 27, Dr. Charles Ross, an oncologist, reviewed the sample of my lymph nodes sent to him by Dr. Jones. Since no cancerous cells werefound, he recommended doing nothing further. He said, "I can authorize radiation or chemotherapy as a precaution, but I don't recommend such treatment when no cancer exists." Naturally, I opted not to receive further treatments, as the doctor advised that it would yield no benefit.

The first night after Dr. Jones removed the cancerous tumor from my colon, I was sedated on morphine, and consequently, my conversations with various visitors were sort of crazy. My wife said that my father in ministry, Pastor W. C. Bunton, stopped by, and my wife said I asked him several times about how the church service was today, and he would answer that they didn't have church service today because it was Tuesday. Then finally, he said church service was fine, and that was that. My roommate for the first few days was a nice young man in his teens or early twenties. His family visited him every day, and they were nice people; however, I don't remember his name.

Rough Thursday Night

2 days after the surgery, I received another blessing from God. Dr. Jones reconnected my digestive system in a manner that would not require me to wear a colostomy bag. On Friday, 3 days after surgery, I was given soft food such as Jello because the hospital staff said that for me to be released from the hospital, I would need to "pass gas" or have a bowel movement or both. Then, just after midday, around 2 PM, a van of about 15 members from Shiloh Baptist Church in Canton, where I started my preaching ministry in 1988, came to the hospital to visit me for the next 3 hours and made me feel like I was important. While I truly appreciated and enjoyed their visit, engaging for that

Henry Leon McNeil

amount of time wore me out. Frankly speaking, I believed it contributed to a subsequent setback I suffered that Friday night.

After feeling sicker than usual, I asked one of the nurses to call ZoAnn Fulp, who just happened to be the nurse in charge of the other nurses on my particular floor. I felt like I had lost that awesome anointed Holy Ghost power that had brought me safely thus far. I believed that the church thought that since the operation went well, I was out of the woods, and consequently, they had ceased praying for me.

When she came to my bedside, I said to her, "ZoAnn, please call the Mt. Olive church members and have them resume praying for me. Tell them that their pastor is not out of the woods yet and continue to pray that the Lord God Almighty will deliver him from the sick bed. "

As that night began to wear on, I became sicker and sicker until around midnight, I felt I was "sick unto death". My stomach was hurting so bad, I literally wanted to die. I asked the nurse to call Dr. Jones, and after she made the call, she said Dr. Jones would be in at 5 AM that morning. Thank God for such a compassionate Surgeon.

A Request to Die

My wife and I were praying for my recovery, but the pain was so severe that I began to pray aloud for God to take me home. In the midst of my suffering, I sensed that God was not going to honor my request to die at this particular time. However, I still needed some relief immediately. So, I prayed to God, asking Him to let me sleep for just two hours to give me some rest from the extreme pain. I requested exactly two hours of rest, and God, in His mercy, answered that prayer. I fell asleep for exactly two hours, no more, no less.

Something even more amazing happened: God revealed to me what the medical problem was. He showed me that the food they had given me was introduced too soon after the intestinal surgery. This led to the onset of what could have been a fatal case of peritonitis. Peritonitis occurs when food processed in the stomach does not properly move to the intestines and becomes toxic. If not addressed, it can be fatal.

When I woke up after two hours, the pain returned just as intense as before. I suffered for another two or three hours until Dr. Jones arrived. When Dr. Jones came into the room, I told him, "I'm not a doctor, but I know what procedure I need you to perform to save my life." Of course, he looked at me in great alarm, but I continued, "You need to pump my stomach because the food they gave me didn't digest properly, and I am about to die because of it." He looked at me in amazement and said, "First, you must be extremely sick to request this. Secondly, I don't know how you know this, but that's exactly what my diagnosis is for your situation." Dr. Jones immediately performed the

procedure, inserting a long tube down my throat to pump my stomach. He removed two one-liter bags of what he described as toxic fluid. He explained to me, "In cases like this, when the food doesn't move from the stomach to the intestines, it causes peritonitis. Your body was becoming poisoned, and if this toxic substance had moved into your system, it would have been fatal." He added, "The only explanation for why you're not dead is that God lined your stomach with something that prevented the poison from penetrating your stomach wall, keeping it contained until we could pump it out."

On Saturday, February 22, I was moved to a new room, where my new roommate was Mr. Jack Reckman (I wrote his name down in my 1998 diary). Dr. Jones required me to stay in the hospital for an extra five days due to the complications I had experienced. Initially, the operation had been scheduled for five days, but my stay was extended to ten days. Each day, Dr. Jones closely monitored my progress, watching to ensure that my digestive system was communicating properly with my intestines. He gradually introduced soft food in small doses, waiting for signs that my body was functioning correctly, specifically, the passing of gas or bowel movements, which indicated recovery.

Released from the Hospital

After many X-rays, blood tests, exams, and constant interruptions throughout the night for tests, my stay at City Hospital finally came to an end. Overall, my hospital stay was pleasant, considering the

circumstances. The medical staff performed their duties with great care, attention, and professionalism. They were observant and effective and, in every way possible, contributed to the healing process. On Friday,

Henry Leon McNeil

February 27, 1998, Dr. Jones came to release me and shared something profound. He said he hadn't expected me to survive my stay, given the two apparent death sentences I had overcome in the past two weeks. First, despite the stage 4 colon cancer diagnosis, God had intervened, and I was now deemed cancer-free. Second, though I had been on the brink of a fatal case of peritonitis, God intervened again, extending my life despite the deadly situation. Dr. Jones acknowledged that no medical intervention could explain why I had survived. "Only God," he said, "has the preeminent authority to alter such medical outcomes." He knew that it was through God's power, not the hospital, that I was healed.

On my last day at City Hospital, Dr. Jones personally wheeled me to the car instead of letting an orderly do it. He wanted to talk to me directly and express how thankful to God he was for my survival. I explained to him that God had indeed intervened, and I was eternally grateful. Dr. Jones agreed and bid me farewell. He was not just my doctor, but became my friend.

Reflection on Healing

There are many diseases that can ultimately end our lives, but we ought to give thanks to God for the skilled physicians He has blessed us with. Through them, He has charted longer paths of life for His creation. While human progress in medicine is remarkable, it is ultimately God who heals, as He is the Creator and Sustainer of life.

Henry Leon McNeil

As of this writing, I have been healed by God for more than **28 years**, and I've been running for Jesus ever since—and I'm not tired yet. It's a wonderful thing to know that we serve a God with unlimited wisdom, knowledge, and power, who is yet merciful, loving, and forgiving. Even though we all have sinned and come short of His glory, by His grace, He grants us extended opportunities to live and continue walking in the newness of life sanctified and set aside for service to Him.

To God be the glory, honor, and praise. Amen.

MEET THE AUTHOR

Henry Leon McNeil has always walked in the favor of God. Having a father as a Pastor gave him a clear example of what living a Godly life was. Once McNeil decided to accept the call into the ministry, He studied under the tutelage of Pastor William C. Bunton. He later began pastoring Mt. Olive Baptist Church, Dennison, Ohio, in 1996. In 1998, McNeil graduated with an M.A. from Ashland Theological Seminary. McNeil has been pastoring for 29 years and has been the pastor of St. John Praise & Worship in Uhrichsville, Ohio, since April 2017. Having lived through segregation, the Jim Crow South, and the Civil Rights Movement, McNeil has a unique and personal perspective that highlights the goodness, grace, and mercy of God. McNeil was compelled to share his experiences to bless others and bring glory to Jesus Christ, our Lord.

Henry Leon McNeil

Henry Leon McNeil